VULCAN'S WORKSHOP

Our word 'volcano' comes from the name Vulcanus or Vulcan.
From at least 1500 BC until about AD 400, the ancient Greeks worshipped a fire god called Hephaistos. The Romans worshipped the same god, and called him Vulcanus. The god was said to own great furnaces, where metals were melted and forged. These were located inside Mount Etna, on the island of Sicily. Etna still sparks like a blacksmith's forge today.

According to one legend, Vulcanus hammered out a magic shield for the Greek hero Achilles. This could reflect the world and everything that was in it.

KRAKATOA, 1883

The volcanic island of Krakatoa, near Java, erupted on 27 August 1883. The sound of the explosions could be heard over eight per cent of the Earth's surface. At least 36,000 people were killed.

A picture taken from space shows a gaping hole where most of Sumbawa island, in Indonesia, should be. The island was blown apart when Mount Tambora erupted and collapsed in 1815.

VESUVIUS, AD 79
DEATH OF A ROMAN ADMIRAL

In AD 104, a Roman writer called Pliny the Younger wrote to the historian Tacitus to describe how his uncle, Pliny the Elder (an admiral and man of letters), had died in AD 79. Pliny the Elder, then aged 56, was stationed with the Roman fleet at Misenum. After lunch on 24 August, his sister Plinia pointed out a large cloud rising above the mountains. Pliny hurried to the harbour and ordered the fleet to be launched. He wanted to launch a rescue mission and, as a scientist, take detailed notes of everything he saw. As he approached the danger zone, ash and stones were raining down from Vesuvius. Going ashore at a friend's house at Stabiae, Pliny ate and rested. However, soon Vesuvius was in full spate and thick, choking ash was everywhere. Pliny suffocated on the shore, where his body was found two days later.

AN ANCIENT CRATER

These cliffs on the Greek island of Thíra or Santorini are crater walls, formed by one of the most massive volcanic eruptions ever experienced. In about 1500 BC, 80 square km (31 square miles) of the island were blasted into oblivion. Clouds of ash and gas drifted over the nearby island of Crete. Thíra erupted again in 1926.

MOUNTAINS OF DOOM

A volcano is an opening in the Earth's crust. Streams of molten rock called lava erupt, or burst out, from the opening. Ashes and rocks may be hurled into the sky. As the lava cools, it hardens and forms new rock. Lava and ash may pile up into a cone, which soon grows into a mountain. Some volcanoes are very violent. Others are more peaceful. Some volcanoes erupt almost all the time, while others only erupt every few hundred or thousand years. Volcanoes which may still erupt are said to be 'active'. Those which were exhausted long ago are called 'extinct'. It is all too easy to write off a volcano as extinct — as scientists have found to their cost.

Only two people out of the 30,000 living in St Pierre, on the island of Martinique, survived the catastrophic eruption of Mont Pelée on 8 May 1902.

Excavations by archaeologists have uncovered Bronze Age towns on the island of Thíra. This is the site at Akrotíri, where fine buildings decorated with beautiful paintings were destroyed by the eruption in 1500 BC.

VESUVIUS THE DESTROYER

Mount Vesuvius rises 1,186 metres (3,891 ft) above the Bay of Naples, in southern Italy.
The height and shape of this volcano has changed many times in history, as the peak has been repeatedly shattered by eruptions and then built up again. The most famous occasion was in AD 79, when the towns of Pompeii, Oplontis, Stabiae and the seaport of Herculaneum were all destroyed. Vesuvius is a serial killer. It erupted with great force again in 1631, in 1779, 1794, 1822, 1872, 1906, 1929 — and most recently in 1944. This painting is of an 18th-century eruption.

FROM THE DEPTHS

To understand how volcanoes work, we need to take an imaginary journey to the centre of our planet. The Earth's centre, or core, is about 3,470 km (2,156 miles) thick. It is made up of an inner layer of solid iron and an outer layer of molten iron, cobalt and nickel. Above the core lies about 2,900 km (1,802 miles) of mantle, made up of many different metals. The lower part of this layer is soft and oozy. The upper mantle is solid, but with pockets of hot, molten rock. The Earth's surface, or crust, is up to 60 km (37 miles) thick beneath the continents, but just 5 km (3 miles) thick beneath the sea. The crust is constantly being created and shaped by restless forces deep inside the planet.

THE ROCK FACTORY

We often think of our planet as solid and unchanging. In fact it has been developing ever since it was formed about 4,600 million years ago. The inside of the Earth acts as a giant powerhouse. The red areas in the mantle (yellow) represent rising hot, molten rock, which forms new surface rock, while old surface rock (blue) sinks and is melted down.

CENTRAL HEATING

At the Earth's core, the pressure is awesome and the temperature is about 6,000 °C (10,832 °F). This causes molten rock, called magma, to surge up through the mantle towards the crust. The magma flows driven by this heat are called convection currents. Where magma bursts through the crust, it becomes the building material for oceanic and continental crust.

Earth's core

This computer image shows the movements of the convection currents around the core. The colours show variations in temperature. Dark blue is the coolest at 303 °C (577 °F). Red is the hottest at 1,200 °C (2,192 °F).

An abandoned truck is engulfed by a great flood of lava after an eruption in Hawaii. The forces that shape the Earth's crust are violent and unstoppable. They are necessary for the survival of the planet, but can spell disaster for the humans who live on its surface.

RIVERS OF FIRE

Once magma has burst out into the air or sea, it is called lava. Here, red-hot lava forms a long, glowing river on Mauna Loa, Hawaii. As it flows, the molten rock slows, cools and hardens to form new rock.

KILAUEA, HAWAII,1990

A smouldering stream of lava from Kilauea Crater, in the south of Hawaii island, inches its way into town. Lava can erupt at temperatures of up to 1,200 °C (2,192 °F). Even as it cools, it is still more than hot enough to set buildings ablaze and melt roads.

Weak spots in the Earth's crust crack open under the force of the magma swelling up below. Sometimes lava oozes out quietly, sometimes it is spewed up with extreme violence. Here, lava from a volcano in the Hawaiian islands spouts and splutters like boiling, red-hot jam.

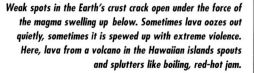

RINGS OF FIRE

We often say that something is as solid as rock. In reality, the Earth's crust is cracked, like a fragile eggshell. The cracked sections, called tectonic plates, are supported by the oozing, soft rocks of the mantle. The unstable borders between the plates are known as 'rings of fire'. These are danger zones for both earthquakes and volcanoes. The convection currents in the mantle make the plates move very slowly. Over the ages, they have caused the continents to drift apart. Where plates move apart beneath an ocean, a rift forms in the sea bed. Magma wells up to form new crust, creating a ridge of undersea mountains on either side of the crack.

Smoke pours through vents called fumaroles, in Hawaii Volcanoes National Park. The Hawaiian islands are a group of submarine volcanoes which have not grown up on a plate boundary, but on a 'hot spot' in the Earth's crust. Hot spots mark areas of great activity in the mantle, where magma punches its way through a tectonic plate.

Lava flows create new rock to fill the gaps, and heat up the sea water. Along cracks called vents, chimneys of minerals build up, spouting out gases which bubble up through the water.

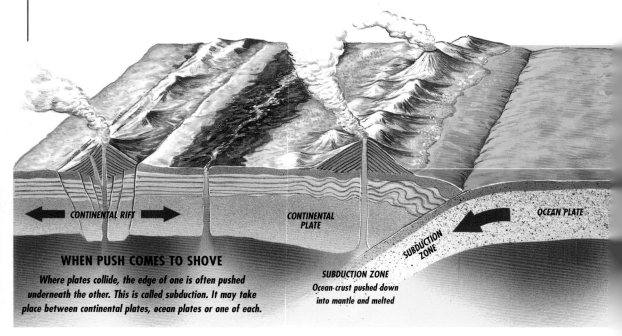

CONTINENTAL RIFT

CONTINENTAL PLATE

OCEAN PLATE

SUBDUCTION ZONE

SUBDUCTION ZONE
Ocean-crust pushed down
into mantle and melted

WHEN PUSH COMES TO SHOVE

Where plates collide, the edge of one is often pushed underneath the other. This is called subduction. It may take place between continental plates, ocean plates or one of each.

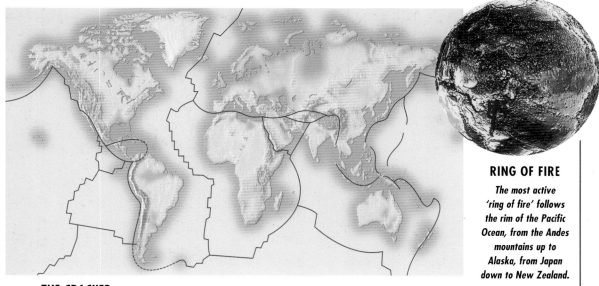

RING OF FIRE

The most active 'ring of fire' follows the rim of the Pacific Ocean, from the Andes mountains up to Alaska, from Japan down to New Zealand.

THE CRACKED PLANET

This map shows the plate boundaries. Most of the world's volcanoes are located along these edges. The divides in the ocean floor are called spreading ridges. Beneath the Atlantic Ocean, the sea bed is moving apart at a rate of about two centimetres (¾ inch) each year. Eastern parts of the Pacific sea bed are opening up at about 20 centimetres (8 inches) per year.

Volcanic activity beneath the sea bed, off the coast of Iceland, created a new island called Surtsey between 1963 and 1966. The new island was named after Surt, who had been lord over the land of fire giants in ancient Norse mythology.

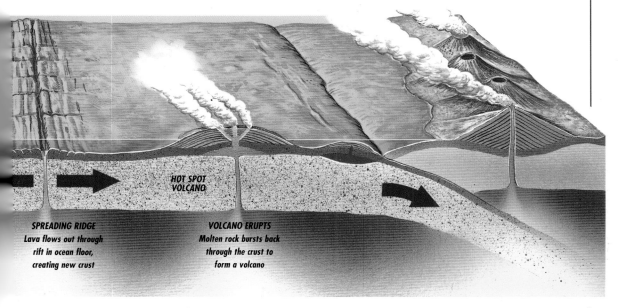

SPREADING RIDGE
Lava flows out through rift in ocean floor, creating new crust

HOT SPOT VOLCANO

VOLCANO ERUPTS
Molten rock bursts back through the crust to form a volcano

Early in the morning of 16 December 1638, the peasants of the Italian region of Campania were herding up their cattle and the priests were in their churches preparing for the festival of Christmas – when Vesuvius erupted again. There had already been months of earth tremors and the crater was gradually filling with lava. At midday, however, two fissures burst open unexpectedly on the southwestern slopes of the volcano. Hot lava flooded out in great rivers. Later that day there were torrential mudslides and new lava flows. Eyewitnesses reported massive falls of ash in the city of Naples. Over 4,000 people perished over the next two days, many in the town of Resina, on the site of ancient Herculaneum.

Sometimes a small crack appears at the side or base of a volcano, leaking gas. Under massive pressure, it may tear open into a long fissure, as happened in the Krafla field in Iceland in 1977. Here we see the two-kilometre fissure releasing large quantities of fluid lava.

ETNA UNPLUGGED

Mount Etna, on the island of Sicily, sits on top of such a large store of rising magma that it is constantly erupting. It rarely has time to build up a large solid plug. This means that the eruptions from its vent are less pressured and less violent than some others.

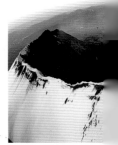

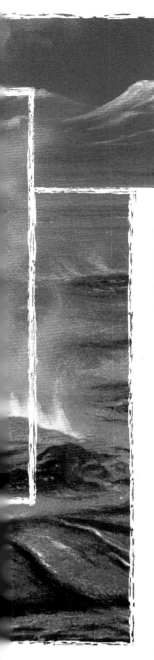

INSIDE THE VOLCANO

Red-hot magma from the Earth's upper mantle rises into great reservoirs or chambers inside the Earth's crust. **Some of the magma seeps between layers of surface rock, to form sills. Some of it may be trapped inside old fissures, to form dykes.** Much of it bursts upwards, to escape through the vents of volcanoes. Repeated eruptions of lava build up steep mountain sides around a powerful central vent. Magma and gases under great pressure also force their way to the surface through secondary vents and fumaroles, leaking gases and steam. The inside of a volcano may be a honeycomb of pipes, vents and fissures. After an eruption, the vents may be plugged as the magma cools and hardens.

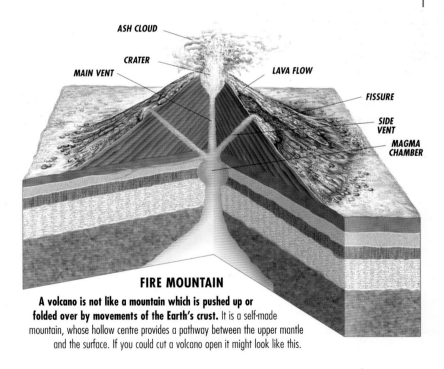

ASH CLOUD
CRATER
MAIN VENT
LAVA FLOW
FISSURE
SIDE VENT
MAGMA CHAMBER

FIRE MOUNTAIN

A volcano is not like a mountain which is pushed up or folded over by movements of the Earth's crust. It is a self-made mountain, whose hollow centre provides a pathway between the upper mantle and the surface. If you could cut a volcano open it might look like this.

THE HOLLOW TOOTH

When a violent volcanic eruption blasts the plug from a vent, it shatters the peak and leaves behind a crater. Some craters still connect with a vent to the magma chamber below, while others are blocked off by new plugs of lava and ash. Some of the most impressive craters are called calderas. These are formed when a massive blast empties the magma chamber, causing the volcano to collapse in on itself.

SIGNS & WARNINGS

AN OMINOUS SILENCE

Like its neighbour, Mount Etna, the island of Stromboli is active most of the time. Its mountain rumbles and grumbles. However, when it falls silent, islanders expect trouble. It often means that rockfalls have blocked the vent and that pressure is building up for a more violent eruption.

Volcanic activity is hard to predict. Even scientists who have been studying a volcano are sometimes taken by surprise. However there are warning signs, some of which have been recognized for thousands of years. There is often an increase in seismic activity (earthquakes and tremors) in the region of the volcano. More and more gases pour out of the crater or from side vents, fumaroles and fissures. They may stink of the mineral sulphur, which smells like rotten eggs. There may be rumbling and other strange noises as magma rises up inside the mountain. Sometimes the whole mountainside bulges from the force of magma, causing buildings to be lifted up and the sea to fall back from the shoreline.

SNAKE WATCH

Reports from many parts of the world suggest that the earth tremors and rising ground temperatures, which precede an eruption, drive snakes out of their crevices and burrows.

MOUNT ST HELENS, 1980

'I AM PART OF THE MOUNTAIN'

The date was 30 April 1980 and Mount St Helens in America's Washington State was declared an emergency area. The most dangerous area was the 'red zone', to which access was forbidden to all but scientists. Property owners in this zone were evacuated, but one 84-year-old man, named Harry Truman, refused to leave his house by Spirit Lake. On 12 May, there was an almighty earthquake, but Harry and his 16 cats stayed put. 'I am part of the mountain,' he told the police patrol. Six days later Harry perished as his home was buried beneath a cliff of ash and stone, as the mountain finally collapsed.

WHITE ISLAND, NEW ZEALAND

One measure of volcanic activity is the plume of smoke rising from its summit. White Island, in New Zealand's Bay of Plenty, offers other clues too. Mud boils and bubbles and whistling jets of steam escape from the ground.

COUNTDOWN: MOUNT ST HELENS

In 1969, American scientists warned that Mount St Helens, a volcano in Washington State, should be carefully watched. From 1975 until 1980, no less than 44 small earthquakes were recorded around the peak. In early 1980, the earthquakes became massive and increasingly frequent. The crater grew and long fissures opened up. The mountainside began to bulge outwards. On 18 May 1980, Mount St Helens erupted in a terrifying explosion (below). This infrared photo (left) was taken the day after.

RUN FOR YOUR LIFE!

People flee from the violent eruption of Vesuvius in 1906. A scientific observatory had been opened on the mountain in 1845. Before the volcano erupted, scientists reported tremors, choking gases and a strange buzzing noise from inside the mountain.

KRAKATOA, 1883
SAILING ON THE RIM OF HELL

On the night of 26 August 1883, a British sea captain, W. J. Watson of the Charles Bal, was sailing through the Sunda Strait between the islands of Sumatra and Java. As he passed the island of Krakatoa, piles of ash and hot stone showered down on to the wooden deck. The crew, fearing for their lives, shovelled the debris into the sea as fast as it fell. The air stank of sulphur and the sailors could hardly breathe. Lightning forked through the sky and the electrical storm known as 'St Elmo's Fire' flickered around the masts. The following morning there was an eerie silence for a time – then at 10 o'clock, the whole island was blasted into the atmosphere with an ear-splitting roar.

THE ROUGH STUFF

Lava rolls down the mountainside. This type is known by a Hawaiian term, aa. It is rough and contains sharp-edged blocks. It is cooler, slower and stickier than other types of lava.

RIPPLES OF ROCK

Black and extremely hot, this lava flow is fast and fluid. It is called by the Hawaiian word pahoehoe. As it cools, it turns into rock with a smooth, rippled surface. Lava which merges under the sea forms rounded blocks called pillows.

SOLID SULPHUR

Volcanic gases contain high levels of sulphur, which solidify as the gases cool to form bright yellow crystals. In some volcanic areas the sulphur is mined, to be used in the manufacture of various products, including rubber and explosives.

BLOWING ITS TOP

A volcanic eruption can blow half a mountain apart. It is an awesome event. The deafening roar from the eruption of Krakatoa in 1883 could be heard on the island of Rodriguez, 4,776 km (2,968 miles) away on the other side of the Indian Ocean. A survivor of the Mount St Helens eruption of 1980 said that it sounded as if the whole mountain had been placed in a giant concrete mixer. Various factors decide just how explosive the eruption will be. Is the vent plugged by cooled magma or debris? If so, the pressure will be greater. Do the volcano's rocks contain water? If so, this can instantly turn into steam, expanding 200 times and smashing through solid rock.

A COLD PLUNGE

On the Hawaiian volcanoes, lava eruptions from the caldera may tower up to 500 metres (1,640 ft). Along fissures, lava may burst out in a long series of lower spouts. It may then start a journey of 30 km (19 miles) or more before cooling. Lava often flows into the sea, where it cools into cliffs of black rock.

Spectators watch in awe as lava pours from the volcanic Galapagos Islands into the Pacific Ocean. Clouds of steam rise from the cold sea water.

HOW THEY BLOW

One eruption may be very different from another. Observers have tried to group volcanoes into various types.

PLINIAN *Gas-rich magma explodes inside the mountain. Cinders, ash and gases are fired up to 30 km (19 miles) in the air.*

PELÉEAN *Gas-rich magma explodes under low pressure. A great cloud of glowing gases, ash and stone rolls down the mountainside like an avalanche.*

HAWAIIAN *After a low-pressure eruption, huge amounts of hot lava flood out and form long flows.*

STROMBOLIAN *Frequent low-pressure eruptions hurl out blocks, blobs of lava and gases.*

VULCANIAN *Periodical higher-pressure explosions hurl out thick lava and very large blocks.*

MT. PELÉE, 1902
BAD ANCHORAGE

On the morning of 8 May 1902, the Roraima, a steamship owned by the Quebec Line, was anchored off the port of St Pierre, Martinique. The crew numbered 47 and there were 21 passengers on board. The Chief Officer, a man called Ellery Scott, later gave an account of what happened. He saw a great cloud roll over the town and the sky turned black. The ship lurched and water rose over the deck. The masts and funnel snapped and the rigging came down. The ship caught fire and there were dead bodies everywhere. Ash and water followed, scalding people and covering them in a cement-like coating. Two hours later, a French ship rescued the 20 or so survivors.

ELECTRIC STORM

As small particles of ash and stone collide and jostle, they crackle with static electricity. Here, lightning plays around Mount Tolbachik, on Russia's Kamchatka peninsula.

THE FALLOUT ZONE

As Krakatoa erupted in 1883, its ash floated down over a vast area of ocean. Some was collected by a ship 1,600 km (994 miles) to the west of the explosion.

MOUNT FUGEN, 1991

This terrifying, smothering cloud of hot gases, ash and smoke is called a pyroclastic flow. Mount Fugen, in the Unzen mountain range in Japan, spewed out lava, ash and hot gases while molten materials rolled down its slopes at 150 km/h (93 mph). Pyroclastic flow can travel at 250 km/h (155 mph).

CLOUDS OF DEATH

During an eruption, clouds of gases such as carbon dioxide and sulphur dioxide escape from the vents. All kinds of materials (known as ejecta) may be hurled high into the air. There are large, solid blocks made of debris or hardened lava; rounded lava 'bombs', still molten inside but with a skin on the outside; small stones or pebbles called lapilli. The smallest ejecta are particles the size of a pinhead. These make up a fine ash which drifts like a deadly snowfall. Ash can be carried high into the Earth's atmosphere and stream around the planet in a long trail.

FLYING INTO THE CLOUD

In 1982, Indonesia experienced a powerful Plinian eruption. The Galunggung volcano pumped a mushroom cloud of gas and ash high into the air. Some 75,000 people were evacuated. Whole villages were buried. A British jumbo jet flew into this ash cloud at a height of 11,200 metres (36,747 ft). The dust choked the engines for over 15 minutes and the aircraft only just managed to land.

Islanders from Montserrat, in the Caribbean, grab cardboard boxes to protect themselves as ash falls from the sky. They were later issued with masks. Mount Chance began to erupt in 1995. In the following two years there were pyroclastic flows and an ash cloud which climbed 10 km (6 miles) into the atmosphere.

DISASTER ZONE

Volcanic forces cannot be tamed by humans. Earthquakes and eruptions can send shockwaves through the ocean, piling up massive walls of water, called tsunamis. Thousands of people were swept out to sea when Krakatoa erupted in 1883. A major risk comes from lava. Earth dams and even bombing by aircraft often fail to divert a strong flow. The molten rock can set forests and buildings ablaze. Gases poison people and ash suffocates them. As the mountainside shakes and collapses, huge avalanches of rock and snow may be released. Snow mixes with soil to create deadly mudslides, called lahars. When Vesuvius erupted in AD 79, the port of Herculaneum was buried under 13 metres (43 ft) of boiling mud.

A TIDE OF MUD

When Nevado del Ruiz erupted in Colombia in 1985, a sea of mud swept through the town of Armero, killing over 23,000 people. To prevent similar disasters, countries such as Japan have built dams and barriers.

A child is rescued from Armero. The best way of saving life is to evacuate people before the eruption. This can be difficult. The volcanoes may be in remote areas and the eruptions may take everyone by surprise.

EMERGENCY RESCUE

Everybody must lend a hand during a major disaster – local people, medical teams, fire-fighters, perhaps the army and airforce too, or international rescue experts. Road and rail links may be destroyed. The eruptions may continue over a long period.

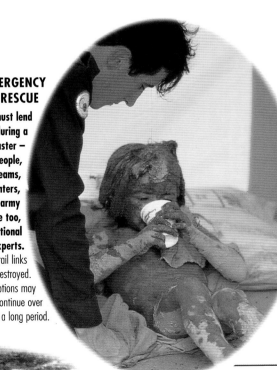

Like a gigantic slag heap, lava creeps over houses on the Icelandic island of Heimaey, after a fissure eruption in 1973.

Ash from the Pinatubo eruption in the Philippines in 1991 clings to the branches of trees. Volcanic eruptions can paralyse towns and cities, close down shops and bring transport to a halt. They often devastate precious forests and destroy crops in the fields, adding the risk of famine to the host of other problems they cause.

HEALTH HAZARDS

Volcanic fallout can cause breathing problems and fire-fighters may suffer burns. Earthquakes can rupture water and gas pipes. Water supplies may be poisoned, spreading disease.

ICE AND FIRE

Heimaey is an island off southern Iceland. In 1973 its volcano, Helgafell, was believed to be extinct. But on 23 January a new fissure blew open, near the town of Vestmannaeyjar. The islanders were evacuated to the mainland, but 300 volunteers remained. While a new volcano grew up around the fissure, an enormous lava flow reached the town and threatened to fill the harbour. Many houses were burnt or engulfed. For four months, the islanders sprayed the lava with sea water, hoping to make it cool and solid.

Volcanic soils can be rich and fertile. On the Canary Islands, grape vines are planted in funnel-shaped holes. The porous rock traps the dew, while lava walls provide shelter from the wind.

RABAUL, 1994
Volcanic activity is a creator as well as a destroyer.
At this site in Papua New Guinea, the volcanic islands have been formed by the subduction of one oceanic plate by another.

HEALING THE SCARS
The Mount St Helens eruption of 1980 reduced whole forests to splintered matchwood.
It emptied lakes and filled them with mud and rubble. It blasted out 275 million tonnes of rock and ash. And yet soon after, plants such as wild lupin and fireweed were pushing up through the layers of ash, and animals were returning to the mountain.

WILDLIFE UNDER THREAT
While some animals soon return to the scene of an eruption, others may find that their habitat has completely disappeared.
In 1998, giant Galapagos tortoises had to be relocated when threatened by a lava flow.

AFTERMATH

The first impression after an eruption is one of total devastation. The hardened lava looks like a lunar landscape. Even the mudslides set as hard as concrete. Peaks have been blown away, and craters have collapsed. Maps of the area need to be redrawn. The release of large amounts of ash into the atmosphere may affect the world's weather for months on end, blocking out the sun. At last, however, life does return to the area. Within 14 years of the Krakatoa eruption in 1883, the fragments which remained as islands had been colonized by no less than 132 species of bird and insect, and by 61 different plant species.

RETURN OF THE PLANTS

How does plant life return to an island after the eruption? Some seeds will be carried there by birds or by the wind. This coconut has floated there on the waves.

THE VALLEY OF 10,000 SMOKES

In 1912, the Novarupta volcano, in remote Alaska, erupted with 10 times the force of Mount St Helens. In its wake it left a new wilderness of ice, rock and steam.

Gunung Agung, on the Indonesian island of Bali, erupted in 1964. However the ancient Hindu temple of Besakih, built on its slopes, still attracts pilgrims and tourists.

TELL-TALE ROCKS

Rocky landscapes give us all kinds of clues about the Earth's crust and how it is formed. Rocks which have been forged by volcanic activity are called igneous ('fiery'). Magma that has seeped up into cracks, and slowly cooled, forms intrusive rocks such as the very hard granites. Magma that has erupted as lava, and then quickly cooled, is called extrusive.

CAPPADOCIA, TURKEY

About eight million years ago, this region was deluged with volcanic ash, cinders and basalt. Over the ages, the rock formed by these minerals was eroded into bizarre pointed columns.

THE GIANT'S CAUSEWAY, NORTHERN IRELAND

It used to be said that the legendary Irish hero Finn Mac Cool built this rocky headland as a road to Scotland. In fact, it is a formation of 40,000 or so symmetrical columns of basalt. They were created by fissure eruptions about 50 million years ago.

LE PUY, FRANCE

This chapel, in southern central France, is built on top of an eroded plug of lava. It is a reminder that many peaceful areas of the world have a violent volcanic history.

RISING ROCKS

Examples of extrusive rock include glassy black obsidian, slabs of basalt and andesite, named after the volcanoes of the Andes. Volcanic activity brings many precious minerals to the surface. Rich deposits of copper, silver and gold surround the Pacific 'ring of fire'. Diamonds, formed in the mantle, are carried to the surface with rising currents of magma.

Pumice is a rock formed from frothy lava that is full of gas. It contains so many bubble holes that it is light enough to float on water.

Diamond Hill is an extinct volcano crater in the heart of Honolulu. Inside the crater is a military cemetery for U.S. soldiers.

CRATER LAKE, OREGON

Crater Lake lies in the Cascade Range, in the western United States. It was formed about 6,600 years ago, when Mount Mazama collapsed, creating a vast caldera. This soon filled with rain and melting snows to form a beautiful blue lake. The little island in the middle is a new volcano in the making.

NGORONGORO CRATER

A giant crack in the Earth's crust runs down eastern Africa. Over millions of years, many volcanoes formed on either side of this Great Rift Valley. One was the mighty Ngorongoro, in what is now Tanzania. When this volcano eventually collapsed, it formed a caldera 20 km (12 miles) across, with a 700-metre (2,297 ft) high rim. The crater floor became a grassy haven for rhinoceroses, lions and zebra.

LIFE AFTER LAVA

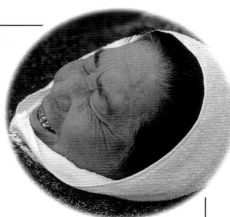

All around the world, there are extinct or inactive volcanoes, craters and calderas. Some of them look extraordinary, but others have become much harder to recognize. Years of erosion may have turned tall peaks into gentle mounds, covered in grass or forest. Craters may have filled with water to become deep lakes. In warm, tropical seas, colonies of little creatures called corals often form chalky structures on the submerged slopes of the volcano. If the inside of the mountain then collapses and sinks down to the ocean floor, these corals will remain in a large ring-shaped reef, forming an atoll.

Volcanic mud is said to have cleansing and healing properties, possibly because of the sulphur, also evident in the warm springs in health spas. This Japanese lady is buried up to her neck, having a volcanic mud 'bath'.

BEACHES OF BLACK SAND

Not all beaches are made up of white or yellow sand. Many tourist destinations have beaches which are black. These include the Greek island of Thíra (left), the Caribbean island of Martinique and the northern coast of Bali. All are volcanic danger zones. Their grains of sand have been worn down from lava flows which have plunged into the sea.

HOW AN ATOLL IS FORMED

FRINGING REEF

A volcano grows from the ocean bed. Corals grow around its slopes.

BARRIER REEF

The volcano collapses and begins to sink.

ATOLL   LAGOON

The volcano vanishes, leaving behind an atoll.

RINGED WITH CORAL

Coral atolls are rings of coral that are scattered across the South Pacific like a string of pearls. They have formed around submarine volcanoes, and teem with marine life.

VOLCANO SCIENCE

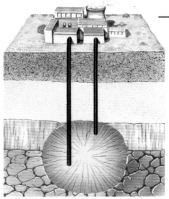

GEOTHERMAL POWER

The heat given out by underground reserves of magma can be harnessed to provide energy on the surface. Heated water turns into steam, driving turbines that generate electricity.

Volcanology is the scientific study of magma and volcanoes. Volcanologists try to find out how the Earth functions. In doing this, they may help to save lives and find new ways in which the destructive power of volcanic activity can be put to good use. Today, some volcanologists can study signals from satellites out in space, which use laser beams to measure plate movements. Others go down in mini-submarines to explore the oceanic crust. Volcanologists may also set off deliberate explosions and record the shock waves which return, in order to find out about the structure of the planet. They may even descend into the terrifying inferno of a volcano's crater.

ON THE BRINK

Volcanologists take samples from active volcanoes. They fill jars with gases and take samples of lava, which they can analyse back in the laboratory. They measure temperatures. A normal thermometer would melt, so they use metal probes called thermocouples, which measure conductivity.

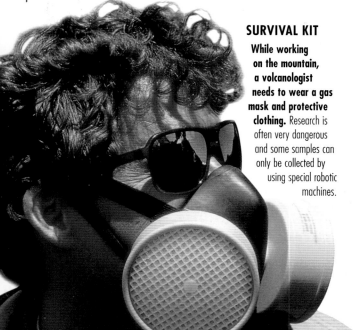

SURVIVAL KIT

While working on the mountain, a volcanologist needs to wear a gas mask and protective clothing. Research is often very dangerous and some samples can only be collected by using special robotic machines.

SOME LIKE IT HOT

Tube worms cluster around a hot vent, in the Galapagos region of the Pacific. In recent years, scientists have used mini-submarines to explore spreading ridges. They have found that bacteria feed on the rich minerals given out, and that these provide food for tube worms and other strange sea creatures.

THE EARTH'S HEARTBEAT

Seismographs are instruments which are used to measure earthquakes and tremors. The information they provide helps scientists estimate the timing and strength of volcanic eruptions. The shockwaves increase dramatically just before a major disaster.

JAPAN, 1952
THE WRONG PLACE AT THE WRONG TIME

On 17 September 1952, the crew of a fishing boat reported strange explosions beneath the sea. Their position was about 400 km (249 miles) south of Tokyo, on the Pacific rim. A volcanic island grew up on the spot, but was promptly blown up in a new eruption. Japanese volcanologists hurried to the scene. The research vessel Sinyo-maru arrived and began to record the dramatic volcanic activity. Another research ship, the Kaiyo-maru, also sailed to the scene. It sailed right over a vent just as it blew. The crew of 22 and seven volcanologists were killed as the ship was blasted apart.

BURIED IN ASH

In Pompeii, the bodies of the victims were destroyed by the hot ash. However they left their shape pressed into the ash before it hardened. By filling these hollows with plaster or resin, archaeologists can recreate the bodies as they were at the time of death.

Plaster-casts show the tragic, huddled figures of Pompeii's victims. They are a moving memorial to all who have suffered from volcanic catastrophe through the ages.

THE FIRST FOOTPRINTS

These footprints were made by ancestors of human beings, about 3,600,000 years ago. They were made in soft volcanic ash, and as this turned into hard rock, the footprints were preserved. They were found at Laetoli, in Tanzania, in 1976.

UNCOVERING THE PAST

One branch of volcano science has been of great use in studying history. When volcanoes engulf the land in ash or lava, they often bury and preserve people's bodies, buildings and streets, jewellery, pots and pans and other evidence of everyday life. When such sites are excavated, it is like opening a time capsule. We find out how people lived long ago. The most famous example is the Italian town of Pompeii, buried by the eruption of Vesuvius in AD 79. The site was first uncovered in 1748. Since then we have discovered how Romans ate, shopped and did business, what their houses were like and even what plants were grown in their gardens.

This fine dolphin jar was discovered on Thíra.

LONG-LOST PAINTINGS

These wall paintings, uncovered at Akrotiri, on Thíra, in Greece, show boys boxing. Other paintings show fashionable ladies, houses and boats. When Thíra was destroyed by a volcano in about 1500 BC, it was part of the fabulous Minoan civilization of nearby Crete.

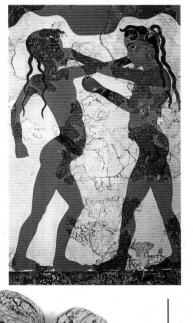

When Vesuvius erupted in AD 79, people were just sitting down to lunch. Food remains that have been discovered include loaves of bread, sausages, walnuts, olives and figs.

VOLCANOES
IN SPACE

THE MAN IN THE MOON

Earth's Moon has dark patterns on its surface, which look like a face. The astronomer Galileo Galilei (1564-1642) called them 'seas'. They are, in fact, plains of basaltic lava which oozed out from fissures and rifts about 2–4 billion years ago.

Where is the biggest known volcano? It can be found, not on Earth – but on Mars. And if we travelled to Venus, we would find volcanoes soaring to heights of 11 km, (seven miles), hardened flows of lava and great slabs of basalt. On Io, a moon of Jupiter, ejecta are hurled from volcanoes at over 1,000 km/h (621 mph). Volcano science can help us discover how other planets and moons have formed around our Sun. At some point in the future, humans may leave our Solar System and settle on other planets. If so, they will have to understand just how those planets were formed and the part played by volcanic gases in the development of their atmospheres.

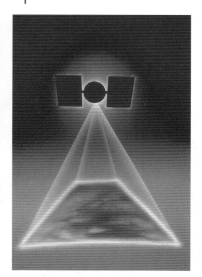

RADAR MAPPING

The Magellan space probe mapped the surface of the planet Venus in 1990-91. It used radar signals to penetrate the thick, poisonous yellow clouds which surround the planet. Venus may be named after the Roman goddess of love, but the surface of this planet is more like hell. It includes baking deserts and towering volcanoes, massive lava flows and hot spots where the rising mantle makes the planet's surface bulge outwards.

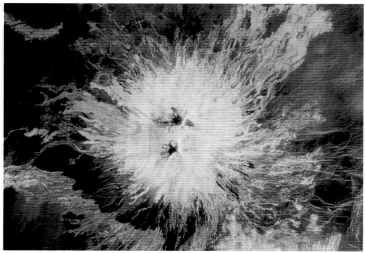

HOT VENUS

Sapas Mons is one of the volcanoes which tower over the plains of Venus. It is 400 km (248 miles) from side to side and 1.5 km (0.9 miles) high. This aerial view is based on a radar image beamed back to Earth from Magellan. At the summit are two eroded tables of rock. Around them is new, rough lava (shown here as bright yellow), giving way to older, smoother flows (dark brown, top left).

MARTIAN VOLCANOES

The volcanoes on Mars are probably extinct, but they are still impressive. This painting imagines the Martian volcanoes Arsia, Pavonis and Ascraeus Mons. The biggest volcano known on any planet, Olympus Mons, rises in the distance.

Olympus Mons is a giant volcano, 24 km (15 miles) high – three times the height of Mount Everest, the highest peak on Earth – and a fantastic 600 km (373 miles) across.

JUPITER'S MOON

You can't get much more volcanic than Io. The gravity of Jupiter (the biggest planet in the Solar System), combined with that of Io's 15 sister moons, stretch and pull at its rocks, keeping them on the boil. There are major eruptions happening all the time, some of which may be as hot as 427°C (800°F). The moon's surface is covered in ejecta and splattered with sulphur, which colours it orange, yellow, red and black. This picture was beamed back to Earth from the Galileo space probe in 1995.

The strange, volcanic world of Io was first glimpsed by the Voyager space probes in the 1970s. This picture, sent back from Voyager 1, shows a bluish gas being pumped out from volcanic vents. With little gravity on Io itself, the gases stream to great heights. They are probably made up of sulphur dioxide, while the dark area at the bottom is probably molten sulphur.

DID YOU KNOW?

The eruption of the island Thíra in about 1550 BC may have given birth to the Greek legends of Atlantis, a civilized land which was lost beneath the ocean waves.

The most volcanic country on Earth is Indonesia, a land of some 13,000 mountainous islands. These possess over 400 volcanoes, of which about 130 are believed to be active. Twenty-four are dangerous enough to be monitored continuously.

The highest active volcano, Ojos del Salado in the Andes range bordering Chile and Argentina, is 6,887 metres (22,596 ft) above sea level.

The Greek philosopher Empedocles (c.490-430 BC) lived on Sicily. He is said to have wanted to disappear from this world suddenly, so that his supporters would believe he was a god. He therefore jumped into the crater of Mount Etna. However the volcano threw back one of his sandals, proving that he had died like a mere mortal.

When Mont Pelée erupted on the island of Martinique, in 1902, 25-year-old Auguste Ciparis was in jail. He was one of only two people to survive in the city of St Pierre. The reason? His cell had very thick walls and its tiny air-vent faced away from the mountain. He later became famous and toured the USA as a circus attraction.

In 1943 villagers at San Juan Parangaricutiro witnessed the birth of a new volcano in their fields. It was named Paricutín. It grew 300 metres (984 feet) high in the first year and then buried the village.

In 1986 an invisible cloud of poison gas rolled out of Nios, a crater lake in the West African country of Cameroon. It killed over 1,500 people.

The northernmost active volcano is Beeren Berg, on the arctic island of Jan Mayen. The southernmost is the impressive Mount Erebus, which towers over the icy wastes of Antarctica.

ACKNOWLEDGEMENTS

We would like to thank: Graham Rich, Hazel Poole, Nicola Edwards and Elizabeth Wiggans for their assistance. Artwork by Peter Bull Art Studio.
Copyright © 1999 ticktock Publishing Ltd.
First published in Great Britain by ticktock Publishing Ltd., The Offices in the Square, Hadlow, Tonbridge, Kent TN11 0DD, Great Britain.
All rights reserved.
No part of this publication may be reproduced, stored in a retrieval system, or transmitted in any form or by any means electronic, mechanical, photocopying, recording or otherwise, without prior written permission of the copyright owner.
A CIP catalogue record for this book is available from the British Library. ISBN 1 86007 110 4 (paperback). 1 86007 118 X (hardback).

Picture research by Image Select. Printed in Hong Kong.

snapping-turtle
guide